Weird Devon

Jonathan Downes
Richard Freeman and
Graham Inglis
of the Exeter Strange Phenomena Research Group

Bossiney Books · Launceston

Dedicated with love to
Lee Holloway
(1945-1999)

First published 2000 by Bossiney Books,
Langore, Launceston PL15 8LD

ISBN 1-899383-38-7
Printed in Great Britain by R Booth (Troutbeck Press), Mabe, Cornwall

INTRODUCTION

The West Country is an ancient and mysterious place with living folk traditions that in many cases predate the Christian era. With the current outpouring of interest in what is broadly known as the paranormal, you need not look any further than our own figurative doorstep if you want to bump into the unknown.

You don't have to go to Roswell, New Mexico, in search of UFOs; you don't have to go to Loch Ness in search of monsters; and you don't have to go to Borley Rectory in search of ghosts, ghouls and spectres. All these things and more can be found in the south-west peninsula of Britain.

Much has been written about the mysteries, the phantasms and the folklore here, but at the risk of being accused of self-aggrandisement we believe this book is unique. This is because we are in a very special position: we are the only people in the West Country (if not in the United Kingdom) who investigate the paranormal for a living.

We finance our research by writing books and magazines, and appearing in television and radio programmes. And because of our high media profile we have been given unprecedented access to a hitherto untapped selection of episodes of high strangeness across the region.

Here we present, almost at random, a selection from our voluminous case files. As they are housed at our office in Exwick on the Exe, they might reasonably be called

The E✗e Files

Jonathan Downes
Richard Freeman
Graham Inglis

THE CASE OF THE UNIDENTIFIED FLYING PIPEFISH

On 19 June 1984, Fred and Elsie Down, both aged 80, of Exmouth, were settling down to watch television when they were startled by a crash which rocked their terrace home. A large block of ice thundered through the roof and into their tiny house, leaving a hole in the ceiling over two thirds of a metre by a third. Fred said:

'When we opened the bedroom door I could not believe my eyes. There was a terrible mess. You could see the sky through the roof. It smashed clean through the slates and broke a rafter. There were also lumps of ice the size of two men's fists lying on the bed.'

Although anomalous falls of ice are often blamed (these days at least) on ice which forms on and then becomes dislodged from the wings of flying aircraft (or more unpleasantly on the frozen sewage discharged from airline lavatories), some objects which descend from the sky are far less easy to explain.

During the summer of 1983, a year before Mr and Mrs Down had their unfortunate accident, Jonathan Downes was working in Exmouth. He was a student nurse on attachment to Stoke Lyne, a hospital (which has since been demolished) for mentally disabled children. He became friends with one of his co-workers there, Mrs Rowley, and he often used to visit her at home in Littleham where he would stay for an evening meal with her and her two young daughters.

One early evening in July the elder of the two girls, who must have been about twelve, came running in, greatly excited to tell him that there were three 'horrid snakes' in the garden. Replete from an excellent meal, her mother and Jonathan wandered outside imagining the girls had discovered a nest of slow-worms, or perhaps grass-snakes. Much to their surprise, there,

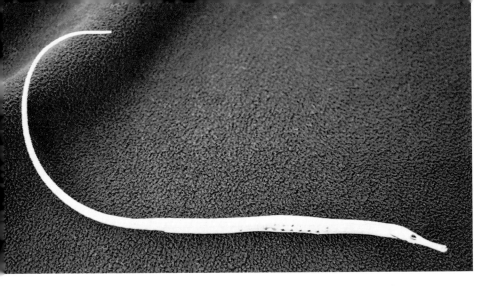

The skeleton of a pipefish – closely related to the seahorse

arranged neatly on the lawn in an almost perfect triangle were three dead, and very desiccated, pipefish.

Several species of pipefish live in British waters and they are not particularly rare beasts, but they are one of the last things you expect to find strewn across someone's lawn in the midst of comfortable suburbia.

Mysterious falls of living creatures (sometimes called 'fafrotskies' – an acronym for 'Fish And Frogs Raining Out Of The Skies') are a well-known phenomenon. Charles Fort had several bizarre and gloriously imaginative theories to explain such strange drops from the heavens. (Charles Fort was an early twentieth century philosopher who throughout his life researched weird occurrences and unwittingly lent his name to the new pseudo-science of 'forteana' – the study of unexplained phenomena.)

His most imaginative idea was the concept of what he called the 'Super-Sargasso Sea'. Just as the Sargasso Sea in the North Atlantic is supposed to be full of shipwrecks and all manner of objects caught up in its gulfweed, so what he termed the Super-Sargasso Sea, an area high above the earth's surface, could be a repository for terrestrial and extra-terrestrial matter. Sometimes it might suck things up; at other times it might spew them back down to earth.

He also formulated the theory of 'teleportation' which involves a force capable of transporting objects and animals from place to place without them having to traverse the intervening distance. This has been used to explain several anomalies, including 'creature-falls' and the strange appearance of various out-of-place animals in spots that logic and conventional zoology suggest they should never be.

Other proposals for such phenomena are numerous. Dr Mike Dash of *Fortean Times* magazine calmly and systematically manages to demolish the most widely accepted reason:

'[An] explanation is often advanced to account for the fall of frogs and fishes: the hapless animals were scooped up from a river or a pond by a passing waterspout, and deposited later some way off. This theory has something to recommend it: for one thing it has long been recognised that a number of such falls really are caused by waterspouts. A whirlwind dropped fish at Quirindi, New South Wales, in November 1913, and fish fell from a waterspout in Louisiana in June 1921.

'Nevertheless, the waterspout hypothesis has weaknesses. There do not seem to be any accounts of rains of tadpoles, nor of smelly mud, broken bottles, old bicycles and the rest of the detritus that normally lurks in ponds alongside the frogs and the fish. And the theory cannot easily explain a number of the most peculiar cases. There are instances of extremely localised falls: at Mountain Ash, in south Wales, a large number of freshwater minnows and sticklebacks fell from the sky in February 1859, covering a rectangle of ground, some seventy-three metres by eleven with fish. (For a long time it was supposed that none had landed outside this extremely limited area, but one recent researcher has shown that a few came down in the surrounding hills.)'

None of these theories explain Jonathan's bizarre brush with a fafrotskie. If the Celestial Sargasso Sea is an innate part of our world, then surely the pipefish would not have been dried when they were found – they should have been fresh and possibly even still alive. The children were playing in the garden all afternoon and were adamant the objects had not been there earlier.

The same would seem to be the case if they had been transported by virtue of a mysterious waterspout. Firstly, there had been no rain for days and, secondly, even if there had been an isolated shower which had managed to evade the detection of Jonathan, Mrs Rowley, both her daughters and the Meteorological Office, and even if this reticent rainstorm had contained a number of fish, then why were both the fish and the grass around them as dry as a bone?

The last theory anyone has suggested is that the fish were dropped into the garden by a passing seabird. Our only answer to that is: if we are forced to hypothesise a mysterious flying piscivorous predator which lives exclusively on desiccated fish, then we are faced with a phenomenon far more bizarre than the one we are examining.

Like so much in this book, fafrotskies in general, fish falls in particular and Jonathan's experience with the three pipefish specifically are just part of the way the universe is. At the moment they are completely inexplicable.

But these were not the only abnormal falls in the Exe Estuary area at that time. During the first week of March 1983, a few months before the encounter with the unidentified flying pipefish, Mrs Rita Gibson of Topsham, Exeter, found a 'scattering' of strange pink beans in her back garden. 'They could not have been thrown,' she says, 'because our house is surrounded by three walls around a courtyard.'

If they fell, where did they come from? The nearest Mrs Gibson could come to identifying the beans, which were larger than rice grains and smaller than orange pips, was to say that they looked like iris seeds. However, iris seeds are orange, not pink, and they are not produced naturally in March. Mrs Gibson commented: 'They don't look like last year's, because they are fresh, not dried out.'

THE CASE OF THE WEIRD
WARBLING WHATSIT

One of the strangest episodes which happened to us during the long hot summer and autumn of 1997 was what a friend and colleague Jan Scarff dubbed 'The Case of the Weird Warbling Whatsit of the West Country'.

Jonathan appeared on our regular BBC radio show, accompanied on this occasion by Jan. Our guest was a zoologist who talked about strange and anomalous appearances of animals in the British countryside. It was an area with which, in his capacity as Director of the Centre for Fortean Zoology, Jonathan was very familiar. We managed to conduct a pleasant if unremarkable show and then returned to Jonathan's house.

As we were sitting there, the telephone rang. It was our guest from the afternoon's show and he had a peculiar incident he wanted to share with us. It appeared that just after we had finished the broadcast one of the listeners telephoned the BBC studios, not realising that our guests habitually join in the show by telephone, and asked to speak to the zoologist.

More by luck than for any other reason, the lady managed to get hold of his telephone number and rang him to tell him a most peculiar story. She lived at Clyst St Mary (a little village just outside Exeter) and had been hearing strange bird calls outside her window in the middle of the night, every night, for the previous five weeks.

The zoologist was convinced the matter was a strictly paranormal one, and outside his own remit, so he passed the case over to us, wished us luck and rang off.

We immediately contacted the lady in Clyst St Mary.

Luckily for us, it transpired she had made a cassette recording of one of these episodes of strange bird calls, and she played it, first of all to Jan and then to Jonathan, down the telephone. It sounded unlike anything they had ever heard before, although it was mildly reminiscent of the weird call of an albatross. But even though albatrosses have been known to venture into the northern hemisphere on odd occasions, the chances of one alighting outside a lady's bedroom window at exactly the same time each night for six weeks and issuing forth unearthly cries for a precise number of times before disappearing was so unlikely as to be statistically impossible.

We decided to visit the scene of these events and, in the words of the characters from a dozen third-rate US TV cop shows, 'stake out the joint'. This we did the following Friday night, accompanied by Dave Hopkins – a keen ornithologist, whom we brought along not just because he is good fun, but because we thought if it *was* some strange bird making these noises then he would be the person in our team most likely to know what sort it was.

According to our witness these sounds always occurred at four minutes past two in the morning, and so we began a long and lonely vigil in the car park of the pub opposite her house. Curiously, the landlord stood outside with us, giving us coffee and telling us ghost stories. Apparently a bar manager several years before had hanged himself, and ever since there had been a string of poltergeist reports and even the occasional sighting. Some of the more superstitious bar staff refused to work after hours alone.

Although we started the evening in high spirits, and an atmosphere of hilarity had prevailed, by the time two o'clock approached we were actually getting quite scared. And when all the owls in the area embarked on hooting and screeching we were most unnerved. Unfortunately we heard nothing remotely

The pub at Clyst St Mary, where the landlord's after-hours tales of ghosts and poltergeists unnerved the research team

akin to the noises that had been played to us.

Feeling somewhat deflated we all went home, but the next day Jan telephoned Jonathan to tell him that, much to her surprise, the lady had reported hearing the same noises as usual during the night, and had even been watching us wandering around the garden at the same time as she had heard them.

This was becoming very strange indeed and when, on the next two nights (Saturday and Sunday), she produced further tape recordings of what was apparently the same noise, we decided there was only one thing we could sensibly do – we had to go to her house, at four minutes past two, wait in her bedroom and see what happened.

Understandably, she was loath to have a bunch of quasi-Fortean researchers trampling around her boudoir and therefore it was only Jan who visited her the following night, laden with paranormal investigating equipment. As time went by, the atmosphere became strained and tense, and by two o'clock you could, in Jan's words, 'cut the atmosphere with a knife'.

Four minutes later the unearthly sounds started. Jan, together with the lady's son Paul, rampaged around her bedroom and eventually found the source of the noise… It was a novelty Japanese watch with an alarm consisting of an electronically-generated crowing cock.

The mystery was solved, but there is an object lesson here for us all. During the days before we knew what had actually caused these sounds, Jonathan appeared on BBC Radio and played the tape, voicing his opinion that here *might* be a genuine paranormal occurrence. As it was, it was nothing of the kind, but if we had not come public in this book with the truth of the matter 'The Case of the Weird Warbling Whatsit of the West Country' could well have passed into the canon of Fortean literature as a genuine enigma.

We wonder how many other prominent cases have equally prosaic explanations.

THE CASE OF
THE BEAST OF HALDON

Around five miles outside Exeter lie the Haldon Hills, a heavily wooded area with an unsavoury reputation – at least two unsolved murders have taken place here. Haldon could well, in fact, be termed a 'window area', that is, a place where many phenomena, especially of a Fortean kind, occur cheek by jowl.

An odd event in this category happened to a friend of ours called John. He was driving with his family through the hills one evening when a dog crossed the road in front of his car. He slowed to avoid hitting it (it appeared to be a golden Labrador), but the animal simply dematerialised in front of the shocked witnesses.

Phantom canines are well-known throughout the British Isles. Every county has its own dog, each with its own name: it's called 'the Bargues' in Yorkshire, 'Skriker' in Lancashire, 'Gallytrot' in Suffolk, and the infamous 'Black Shuck' in Norfolk.

Fox Tor Mire, near Princetown on Dartmoor, believed to have been the model for the Great Grimpen Mire in the Sherlock Holmes adventure, The Hound of the Baskervilles. *Conan Doyle based his novel on the many tales of phantom dogs in Devon folklore, such as the 'Wisht Hounds' or 'Yeth Hounds', a pack of which hunted the moors at the command of their master the Devil, chasing down lost souls...*

Generally these beasts are described as donkey-sized, jet black animals with fiery red eyes. Some however are white, but nonetheless menacing for it. Their appearance used to be said to be a portent of death, and modern witnesses speak of an overwhelming terror which seems to emanate from these 'hell hounds'. They are also sometimes accompanied by a foul stench rather like sulphur.

In the West Country some phantom dogs are considered to be benign rather than evil, which puts the West at odds with the rest of the country. There is a belief that they are the ghosts of lost sailors, and that they will protect women and lead home those lost in moorland fog.

The pet cemetery on the Haldon Hills. Home-made crosses and DIY tombs poke at odd angles among the mist-shrouded trees. Everything, from dogs, cats, and rabbits to boa constrictors and even a pony are all buried here

Black dogs are often associated with certain stretches of road – one haunts the old road through Morchard Bishop, above Copplestone. There is even a hamlet called Black Dog about a couple of miles north-east of Morchard Bishop. Here every November a festival called 'the walking of the black dog' occurs. A huge effigy of the ghostly hound is carried four miles through the lanes he is supposed to haunt, accompanied by crowds of people singing, dancing, and waving lanterns.

And from dogs to pets in general. Nestled in a mossy forest glade in the Haldon Hills is an unofficial pet cemetery. For years this has been the last resting place of many faithful friends of local folk.

In recent years this already eerie place has become even more unsettling. Graves have been disturbed by something interested in flesh, not trinkets (from time to time grave robbers of a human kind callously take the sentimental items buried with the animals). And some folk have caught glimpses of a strange creature stalking the cemetery at night. One such witness was Colin Yeo, a former police marksman.

Whilst driving along one of the narrow back roads that traverse the area he saw a huge dark-brown cat-like animal bound out of the shadows and across the road in front of his car. It was about 1.8 metres long. On a separate occasion, when walking his dog, he disturbed the beast whilst it was in the act of digging up a body. Another witness told us that an animal also stalked him and his dog a stone's throw from the graveyard.

As the number of sightings mounted up, the Exeter Strange Phenomena Research Group decided to carry out an investigation in early 1998. The main suspect in the case was *Felis concolor*, the puma. This large cat is found throughout the Americas, from Argentina to Alaska. It used to be readily available as a pet in the UK, and a surprisingly large number were kept as such. However, in 1976 the Dangerous Wild Animals Act passed through parliament and the legislation made having such animals at home difficult. As a result, rather than allow their beloved pets to be destroyed, many owners turned their charges loose. So, in the wilds of Britain, with no competitors, these cats prospered and bred. Feral populations now live in many parts of the country.

Our plan was to lure a puma into camera range and for help we turned to an old friend, Ellis Dawe, the director of the Dartmoor Wildlife Park – a zoo with the finest collection of cats in Britain. The park has five pumas of its own. Mr Dawe has seen wild pumas come down from the moors on several occasions and stalk around the zoo's puma enclosure when the females are on heat.

Even in captivity, puma can be quite elusive

Mr Dawe was good enough to let us into the cats' enclosure to collect their droppings in the hope that these would attract the wild pumas in Haldon. It is testament to the puma's unaggressive nature towards humans that, although many of the research group entered their pen, the animals remained calm. They also demonstrated their renowned elusiveness and were hard to see even within the confines of their enclosure – one suddenly leapt down out of what seemed to be nowhere (it was actually from a tree) right over Richard's head, and another came within centimetres of Graham's hand.

A couple of hours later we sprinkled the fresh dung around the pet cemetery. We had also procured some offal and used it to lay down 'scent trails'. This involved dragging the meat through the woods in a hessian sack, leading back to the graveyard. Sand traps were constructed too. These consisted of a piece of meat laid in the centre of an area covered in very fine sand. Any animal taking the bait would leave diagnostic foot prints in the sand.

Then we waited, together with Toby, the Centre for Fortean Zoology's dog, during a very long, very dark night. But nothing slipped out of the shadows. The beast resisted the smell of female company and a free supper, and we saw nothing. The sand traps were empty of bait, and contained only the foot prints of foxes and buzzards.

Ah well, a puma's territory can cover over twenty square miles, and the animal (whatever it is) is still seen regularly. The case of the Beast of Haldon and the cursed hill is still very much open.

Ellis Dawe, the director of the Dartmoor Wildlife Park, with casts of big cat footprints

But before closing this chapter on Haldon, we feel we must mention a further oddity, albeit not perhaps of a terrestrial kind. One night in April 1997, at about 11.00 pm, Yvonne Jackson was sitting in a car on the top of Haldon Hill with her boyfriend and another young man when they saw a semi-circular object with three rows of lights, making approximately twenty lights in total of various colours flickering and rotating.

The object was at an elevation of approximately fifty or sixty degrees and seemed to be hovering in the sky over Teignmouth Estuary. A few months later Yvonne described it to us rather picturesquely as 'bobbling around', but when we spoke to her some time after that she could only say 'It was absolutely enormous...'

Her boyfriend's friend gave details of the sighting to the local police, who said they'd had lots of reports of flickering lights. However, the police at Teignmouth were less helpful when we got in touch with them and could only comment that reports of such incidents had to remain confidential. This wasn't really true: when contacting other community policemen over the following months, we discovered that in most cases they were quite happy to give us information, although they often preferred it to be 'off the record'.

And from that case of an unidentified flying object to another.

THE CASE OF THE HIPPY
WHO SAW ALIENS

Trish Lovelock was a traveller for the best part of eighteen years, and spent six of those years with her old bus parked up on an ancient Celtic burial mound. She became a traveller, or so she claims, essentially because of her deep dissatisfaction with the ethos of the late twentieth century, and she was convinced that by adopting a nomadic and open air lifestyle she could get closer to the answers to the fundamental questions of life.

She now lives in a tiny stone cottage deep in the heart of Bodmin Moor and is the first to admit that her experiments in an alternative lifestyle didn't really work. In the summer of 1997 she told us, 'I suppose I'm still searching for the answers, but maybe that is my fault rather than because of flaws in my chosen lifestyle.'

Sipping tea, in a neat sitting room, she related in a surprisingly matter of fact voice some extraordinary experiences in her life during her years on the road. These involved Unidentified Flying Objects, entities which closely resembled alien 'Greys', and even events which seem very closely aligned to those reported by some survivors of the 'abductee experience'.

'Now, nearly 40 years old, and a grandmother twice over, I live in the relative safety of an old stone cottage in a tiny village in Cornwall. I am no closer to finding out whether or not "the truth is actually out there", but I do know that the universe is a very strange place, and that we are far from knowing all the answers!

'During the early 1980s I was at a festival with a number of other travellers when I saw something which has since become one of the most familiar images of contemporary UFOlogy.

'We were lying on the grass outside our tents, gazing up at the night sky. Out of the corner of my eye I saw a bright light, high above us. As I focused on it I could see that it was a huge, white triangle of light which appeared to be many metres across, hovering high above the ground. I pointed it out to my companions. One of them saw it with me, but he just took it in his stride.

'We watched this wondrous phenomenon for about ten minutes as it hung motionless in the sky above us. Then it moved off to one side and vanished as quickly as it had arrived. (I would like to stress here that I was perfectly sober.) The archetypal "triangular space-craft" has since become a common icon, and I take more than a little pride in the knowledge that I was witness to such an event long before they became commonplace.'

A more sinister series of events took place in the summer of 1989 whilst Trish and her family were living at a travellers' park-up at Stibb Cross in North Devon.

'My boyfriend at the time had a series of encounters with what he described as a "little grey alien", very similar to those depicted on the front cover of Whitley Streiber's book *Communion.*

'One night he was driving along the road, together with my daughter Jenny who was about eight years old at the time. She remembers seeing a ball of white and yellow light "about the size of a football" suspended in the road in front of them. With no time to stop, they drove straight through the light which appeared to enter the car and go straight through it. She remembers how the light felt strangely warm, although she can remember suffering no ill effects from her experience.

'My recollections of Mark's account at the time, however, are somewhat different. I remember him telling me how, terrified, he reversed away from the light and drove away as fast as he could, and that another car on the same road did exactly the same thing and both cars reversed down the road as fast as they could.

'My boyfriend started to suffer from unusual tiredness and used to go to bed extremely early. Each morning when he awoke he had strange triangular red "burns" on his arms, and I think, once, on his neck.

'Although they appeared to be burns, these regular isosceles triangles did not blister and seemed not to cause him any pain. He was convinced these marks were somehow linked to an alien entity he nicknamed "George". He even claimed that "George" had sat in the car with him one night and attempted to communicate with him.

'A Druid friend of mine, known as "Badger", was driving my car one night when she had a momentary sighting of what appeared to be a very similar entity in the rear view mirror. This activity seemed to be inextricably linked to the location where we were camping, because when we left Stibb Cross we seemed to leave "George" behind us.

'Jenny also saw what she described as little figures running off into the undergrowth on a number of occasions, although now she has half convinced herself they were rabbits or birds going about their natural business.

'Other weird things happened at the same time. On a number of occasions we saw strange flickering lights in the night outside our bus. On one night a car, which was parked outside, rolled downhill into a convenient bush, but although the ground was wet there were no tyre marks.

'A few days later a similar incident happened, but this time the events were even more inexplicable as the car seemed to roll uphill into a muddy ditch from which it had to be pulled out by a tractor!

'Another day we found a burnt-out car in the middle of the moor. The strangest thing about that was there were no scorch marks on the ground around the vehicle and it seemed as if it had somehow been transported to the place where we found it.

'My boyfriend became obsessed with the imagery of the archetypal Grey after his encounters with "George", and for months afterwards he made tiny alien heads out of modelling clay. Long after we left Stibb Cross, the psychic reverberations of that sinister spot haunted our whole family, and even now the memories leave us all with a chill down the back of our necks.

'I would rather not venture an opinion as to the nature of the things I have seen. Whether or not they are beings from another part of the galaxy, from another dimension, from another reality, I don't know. I have a sneaking suspicion they are just part of the way that things are, and that they can be experienced by anyone who turns their back upon the city for a simpler existence beneath the stars.'

THE CASE OF THE OLD SOLDIERS
(WHO WOULDN'T FADE AWAY)

By anybody's standards Common Moor at Stibb Cross is a most peculiar place, and Trish Lovelock and her ex-boyfriend are not the only people to have experienced strange goings on there – we have numerous reports from people who have visited the area. We have ourselves been to this desolate stretch of gorse and peat on many occasions, and can confirm that the place does indeed have an oppressive and sinister atmosphere.

One person who telephoned us following a radio programme we broadcast on ghosts described seeing what he was convinced was a 're-playing' of a skirmish from the English Civil War on this very stretch of moorland. The man related unnatural events that befell him around thirty years ago. Whilst cycling across the moor one October afternoon he became aware of an acrid smell…

'Then something caught my eye. It seemed that several hundred oddly dressed men were fighting in a shallow depression about a quarter of a mile to my left. I assumed they were making a film and crept closer.'

Hiding himself behind a bush, he quickly realised that it was no film:

'The men were shooting at each other with muskets. These seemed very inaccurate, with only a few shots finding their targets on either side. I recognised the costumes from my history lessons at school, and knew they were Roundheads and Cavaliers. The Roundheads had groups of pikemen who moved and acted as one. They rushed forwards with the pikes held down – it reminded me of a huge porcupine! The pikes were so long that the swords of the Cavaliers could not reach the Roundheads.

'When you see a man impaled on a spear during a film on television he dies quickly, but the skewered Cavaliers that I "saw" that day were thrashing and writhing on the wooden spears. Some kicked so violently, they pulled the pikes from the hands of their killers!'

Terrified that one of the combatants should turn and see him, he ran back to his bike.

'It was only when I reached my bicycle that I realised I hadn't heard any sounds, although I had been standing in what appeared to be close proximity to a pitched battle! No sounds of musket fire, no screams of dying men, no clash of steel upon steel. I rode home like a mad man and did not tell a soul for almost thirty years. To be truthful, I doubted my own sanity!'

The most credible explanation for the way that this and other historical events can seemingly be replayed over and over again across the centuries is known as 'The Stone Tape Theory'. Graham McEwan describes it best in his *Mystery Animals of Britain and Ireland* (1986):

'…the theory being that events, especially if violent or tragic, can leave a recording on their immediate surroundings. The energy is stored, and may be reactivated, maybe many years later, when the conditions are right. The presence of living people may be a requisite, for example. I believe the stone tape hypothesis received its name after the BBC broadcast a television play on this theme by Nigel Kneale, called *The Stone Tape*. The theory, however, is perhaps most notably associated with author and researcher TC Lethbridge.'

In the absence of a better explanation this will have to do. It is interesting to note, however, that this incident is far from being unique in the annals of West Country weirdness. According to West Country ghost expert Mike Evis:

'The ghosts of several hundred men haunt an almost anonymous field tucked away in a corner of the village of Westonzoyland, near Bridgwater. This is the site of the last battle ever fought on English soil – the Battle of Sedgemoor in 1685. The Duke of Monmouth's attempted rebellion had begun with his landing at Lyme Regis. From there he raised men, arms and rebellion throughout the West Country. Monmouth's "pitchfork" army (so called because of its heavy peasant following) finally met forces loyal to the King at Sedgemoor and were completely crushed. Many of the participants were hanged following Judge Jefferys' "Bloody Assizes".'

A north Devon man who has asked us to respect his anonymity telephoned us after another episode of the radio show 'Weird about the West'. He told us about something which he, too, had experienced as a child. He had also seen what appeared to be a 'replay' of a Civil War skirmish in a field between Clovelly and Hartland.

Jonathan was brought up in this area during the late 1970s and knows the field well. He was friends with the children of the farmer who owned it and, whilst he was not aware of any local stories about sightings of a battle there, he was told by his friends that their grandmother, who lived in a cottage on the farm, had regularly seen the ghost of a Cavalier who reputedly haunted the area.

Great Torrington, a pretty little market town in North Devon and not far from Stibb Cross, is also a well-known site of what appear to be ghosts from the English Civil War.

Taking place in the mid 1600s, this war is probably most famous for the names of the participants – the Cavaliers and the Roundheads. Various parts of the country saw fighting between the two sides, and Great Torrington had its fair share, coming under attack from the Roundheads. The Cavaliers fell back to fighting in the narrow streets, but their attempts to preserve the town were thwarted when their gunpowder supply, stored in the church, suddently exploded.

This event would seem to have had unexpected repercussions in modern times. Andrew Green, one of Britain's foremost chroniclers of ghost stories, writes:

'In 1976, Joan White of Chatham with her husband and two children stayed in the small cottage which had once served the village as a public house. She read with interest in a tourist brochure that "a disastrous fire all but destroyed the town in the seventeenth century", but no other detail was provided.

'On their last day Mrs White was woken "just before dawn" by a "peculiar light in the bedroom. It swung from side to side", she said, "moving from the back wall to the front. It was soft and golden, swinging in rhythm. When it reached the bedroom floor I heard a woman's voice shouting in a language I could not understand. Then two or three began to protest, and then came the noise. It sounded like a group of motor-cyclists roaring past the house, the noise increasing with great speed in a roaring crescendo. Then suddenly it stopped, leaving Devonshire peace to reign."

'At breakfast her teenage children complained that they too had heard the noise. "It sounded like a lot of motor-cyclists speeding up the tiny street", or, one might suggest, an explosion of gunpowder. But the streets were empty of humans at the time.'

This incident in Great Torrington's history was also alluded to in a children's book *Simon* by Torrington author Rosemary Sutcliffe, whose writings are fondly remembered by the three of us as being very helpful in explaining the events of the Civil War in the West Country.

If the Stone Tape Theory is correct, then the amount of psychic anguish caused during a bloody civil war, and especially one that spawned some dreadful atrocities like the destruction of a church full of wounded soldiers, would be beyond belief. If indeed an outpouring of emotion can somehow be 'recorded' and 'replayed' at a later date, then Great Torrington would seem to be a perfect site for this to happen.

The fact that these events are witnessed on a regular basis here would seem to be a vindication of the theory.

THE CASE OF THE MEDIUM WHO LOST HER MARBLES

In the early summer of 1997 we received a telephone call late one night from a very frightened woman living just outside Newton Abbot. She told us that, for several weeks, every time she had gone into her front porch she had found one or more marbles (of various designs) on the doormat. At first she thought nothing of it, assuming it was nothing more than a bizarre (and slightly surreal) prank by local children. But over the next few weeks the marbles continued to appear. Becoming annoyed, she decided to attach a metal box to her letter box which would collect her mail, but wouldn't allow it, or anything else, to drop to the floor.

The marbles, however, continued to be deposited on her doormat, and what was even more uncanny was that the arrival of these things was preceded, on each occasion, by a rattle at the door. Several times she was in her sitting room, heard the tell-tale rattle and looked out of her front window. There was never anyone there, but invariably there were one, two, and on one occasion five glass marbles on her doormat.

By this time she was badly frightened and so she consulted a local psychic. The psychic duly arrived, had a cup of tea and proceeded to go into a trance. In a voice ridden with foreboding, she informed the lady that there was 'an unquiet spirit' in residence and that, for reasons of its own, it was trying to contact the household by means of these marbles.

24

On being questioned further, the psychic announced that this unquiet spirit was that of a small child who had died and whose spirit was stuck in limbo. The psychic then picked up one of the marbles, screamed (claiming it was red hot), and started to mutter in some arcane language. Shortly after, she came out of her trance, took her twenty-five pounds consultancy fee and left.

By this stage the lady was both terrified and very upset. A few months earlier, her daughter had given birth to her first grandchild – a boy who had been stillborn – and she was now convinced the 'unquiet spirit' to which the psychic had referred was that of her dead grandson.

She then telephoned us.

The materialisation of inanimate objects (usually called 'apports') under mysterious circumstances is a fairly well-known (if rare) phenomenon, often associated either with mediumship circles or with poltergeist activity, and we were initially quite excited by this case. However, years of experience have taught us that things like this are never quite what they seem, and so, although we promised that if necessary we would drive to Newton Abbot to investigate the case in person, we first asked for the telephone number of the self-styled psychic.

When we telephoned 'Mystic Marjorie' (no, that isn't her real working name but we have enough respect for the laws of libel not to reveal her identity further), she was less than helpful. Belligerently she told us that she and her spirit guides had the whole affair under control, and that we were only going to do an immense amount of damage if we became involved. She then tried to charge us a twenty-five pound consultancy fee, before slamming the telephone down.

We then rang the 'marble lady' (as we had begun to think of her), to make an appointment to visit her. She wasn't in, but her son was and he was shaking with hysterical laughter.

The mystery had been solved.

Apparently, a few weeks earlier she had bought a fancy roller blind at a car boot sale (incidentally the same one at which she met 'Mystic Marjorie'). She had duly installed it in her porch, where it covered a little dormer window which she kept open to provide fresh air.

The roller blind had been weighted with marbles, and there was a tiny hole in the end of the weighted section. Every time the wind blew, the roller blind moved, shedding marbles in its wake, and the rattle on the door was nothing more than the sound of them bouncing off the metal letter holder she had fixed on the inside of her letter box.

He apologised for wasting our time and put the phone down.

We found the whole affair mildly amusing, apart from the obvious and grave distress that had been caused to the lady (and presumably her daughter) by the so-called 'psychic', who obviously had about as many magic powers as our cat Carruthers. For reasons of her own, not entirely unconnected with the twenty-five pound 'consultancy fee', she had re-opened relatively fresh emotional wounds and caused the family completely unnecessary distress.

The moral of the story is: never buy any cheap roller blind (or any expensive psychic) that you find in a car boot sale.

THE CASE OF THE STRANGE APES

R D Blackmore described a tribe of lawless vagabonds, 'The Doones', in his famous novel *Lorna Doone* (which, incidentally, has at least one other episode of interest to the Fortean zoologist – a sub plot loosely based around the semi-legendary 'white bird' of Oxenham Manor).

Going well back into historical times and even within the past three hundred years, there have been strong traditions of tribes of naked wild men living in the remotest parts of Dartmoor. It is also said that one tribe of semi-wildmen lived in the parish of Nymet Rowland for about two hundred years. But it's likely that

On these rocks above Lustleigh Cleave one witness stated she had seen a family of 'cave men', either naked and covered in hair or wrapped in the shaggy pelts of wild animals

the Doones were merely based on a group of highly organised vagabonds and criminals who lived on the Devon-Somerset border on Exmoor.

As well as accounts of wild men, there are a number describing entities whose nature seems far more analogous to some of the stranger apes reported around the world. In the steep-sided lanes around the village of Colebrooke, for example, a phantom monkey is said to lurk. The beast supposedly has red fur and attacks people.

The Devon folklorist Theo Brown gathered a number of such stories, including one chilling recollection by a friend of hers who had been walking alone at dusk near the ancient earthworks at the top of Lustleigh Cleave on the extreme eastern side of Dartmoor.

Lustleigh Cleave is an extraordinarily strange place, and it appears to be one of those 'window areas' where unexplained incidents and anomalous phenomena seem to take place on an almost monotonous basis. We have reports of sightings of a ghostly Tudor hunting party, mysterious lights in the sky, and even the apparitions of a pair of Roman centurions.

Theo Brown's friend clearly saw a family of 'cave men', either naked and hairy or wrapped in the shaggy pelts of wild animals, shambling around the stones at the top of the cleave.

In south Devon, between the towns of Paignton and Brixham, lie Churston Woods. These woods have long been of interest to us, because of the sightings of mysterious small carnivores which could be a relict population of Beech martens (a species thought extinct in Britain since the last Ice Age).

Fifteen separate witnesses over a six-week period in August/September 1996 reported seeing what they described as 'a green-faced monkey' running through the woods. Whilst some of the descriptions were very vague, most of them included a tailless, hairy animal between 1.2 and 1.5 metres tall, with a flat, olive-green face.

Although there are primates with 'green' faces (for example the olive baboon and some of the west African vervet monkeys), none of these correspond in the slightest to the descriptions of a humanoid or chimp-like creature which was seen both swinging through the trees and running through the woods. Perhaps the old 'fairy tales' of trolls under the bridge are not too far from the truth.

THE CASE OF THE SEA SERPENT
THAT NEARLY WAS

Sea serpents around the Devon coast have largely been over-shadowed by Morgawr, the Cornish sea dragon – a snake-necked, humped-backed, reptilian Nessie lookalike seen consistently since the eighteenth century. However, looking through our files we note that there have actually been many dazzling reports of all sorts of sea creatures from Devon.

Richard Freeman preparing to conjure up sea serpents. If it had not been for the baleful presence of a large and intrusive TV crew, the ritual would almost certainly have been more successful...

Richard Freeman is a ritual magician with a deep rooted interest in dragons, and a few years ago had been planning his own serpent-raising ritual. He was approached in July 1998 to perform just such a conjuration for a local television company who were filming a documentary on sea serpents. (The celebrated wizard and surrealist painter Anthony 'Doc' Shiels has summoned sea dragons with ritual magic on many occasions. He has performed monster raising rites at Loch Ness, several Irish lakes, Falmouth bay, and Parsons beach. Many witnesses and several photographs of these great wyrms stand as testament to both his occult skill and the existence of these saurians.)

Resplendent in ritual robes and wielding his ritual sword,

Richard duly obliged. Unfortunately, high magic and TV companies do not make the best bedfellows. The ceremony was halted, restarted, held up and re-shot from different angles. Cries of 'Can you just evoke those dragons of the western quarter one more time for sound?' and such became all too familiar. In short, the ritual was never really carried out; it was just a set piece for the cameras. But it seemed his shenanigans did have some effect…

In August 1998, just one month later, two 15-year-old Topsham girls were walking along Saunton sands when they noticed an odd shape in the water. As it drew closer, they could make out what appeared to be a snake-like head and neck, and a large humped body. With shaking hands they pulled out a pocket camera and took a snap of the object.

Within days the Exeter Strange Phenomena Research Group was called to the offices of the *Express and Echo* – the local newspaper which was about to run the story. They wanted a trained zoologist to examine the picture before they went to press.

Wearing the guise of an experienced zoologist rather than a magician, Richard took a close look at the monster. The creature did indeed bear a resemblance to the classic picture of a sea serpent, but something worried him. The animal's outline seemed very irregular and, after consideration, he was forced to dismiss it as a hoax. A couple of days later he was vindicated, the sea monster turning out to be nothing more esoteric than an oddly shaped log.

A fake monster-raising ritual seemed to have spawned forth a fake monster!

However not all monster sightings can be explained so easily. As a boy in the 1970s, Richard often holidayed with his family in Devon. One summer, when he was aged about nine, his grandfather fell into conversation with a retired trawler man living in Goodrington. The old man recounted his life as a fisherman and one particular incident which had stuck forcibly in his mind.

Some years previously he and his crew were trawling off Berry Head. The seas off this part of the coast are amongst the deepest waters around Britain. Such are the depths of this section of the English Channel that the area is commonly used to 'scuttle' or sink old ships. The drowned wrecks have made an artificial 'reef' which attracts vast amounts of fish. Good catches are therefore almost guaranteed and the area has become a popular place to drop nets.

One night the crew had trouble lifting the nets and began to worry that they had got them entwined about a rotting mast. Soon, though, they felt some slack and they began to haul them up. The men thought their catch must have been a particularly good one, so heavy were their nets, but as they were drawn closer to the trawler's lights a frightening sight took shape. The crew had not caught hundreds of normal sized fish, but one gigantic one.

'It was an eel, a giant eel. Its mouth was huge, wide enough to have swallowed a man. The teeth were as long as my hand.' Even now Richard still remembers the words of the ancient fisherman and is convinced this was not a tall story designed to entertain gullible tourists.

'While it was still in the water it was buoyed up, but as soon as we tried to pull it on board the nets snapped like cotton and it vanished back down. I was glad it went. I've been at sea all my life, but I've never been as scared as I was that night. I can still see its eyes, huge, glassy...'

The man couldn't determine what length the beast was, as it had been coiled in the nets. We can, however, make an educated guess. We don't know what the breaking strain is on the average trawler's net, but logic dictates that it must be several tons, so this must have been a truly massive animal. In order to have a mouth wide enough to swallow a human, a standard conger eel would need to be scaled up to around fifteen metres.

This was only one of the legion of such tales from Devon's

rocky coastline. In the late 1930s a creature described as a 'giant conger eel' terrorised the south coast of Devon, frightening fishermen and tourists from Berry Head to Plymouth. Events such as this clearly show we cannot confine monsters and dragons to story books and camp fire tales.

British waters are becoming warmer. Sub-tropical species such as sunfish, triggerfish, and even the great white shark are moving into our seas. Should we be so surprised if the Great Sea Serpent also returns? It rather makes you reconsider that little paddle in the briny, doesn't it?

EPILOGUE

The life of a paranormal researcher might not be quite as romantic as you would think. The daily high adventure and life or death struggles with the minions of darkness, as portrayed on the screen, are noticeably lacking. We don't have government backing or a limitless supply of funds and, unlike us, our television counterparts are never plagued by overdrafts or run down cars.

Where we do get one over on them is knowing that the real world is so very much stranger than the silver screen. Trite, shallow explanations of government cover-ups and beings from outer space are a pale shade of some of the things that really are 'out there'. We have but scratched the veneer of the paranormal phenomena of Devon. Look close enough and the cosy picture postcard image of this county will melt like an ice lolly on a summer's afternoon.

…and yup, the truth really *is* out there!

If you would like to contact the Exeter Strange Phenomena Research Group, telephone (01392) 424811 or visit their web site at http://www.eclipse.co.uk/cfz/esp.htm.